cooking with **apples & pears**

Laura Washburn

photography by Peter Cassidy

RYLAND
PETERS
& SMALL

LONDON NEW YORK

For I.P.

**Design, prop styling, and photographic
 art direction** Steve Painter
Commissioning Editor Julia Charles
Production Controller Maria Petulidou
Art Director Leslie Harrington
Publishing Director Alison Starling

Food Stylist Linda Tubby
Index Hilary Bird

Author's acknowledgments
Thanks to everyone at Ryland, Peters & Small
for putting together such a winning team.
The photos, props, and food styling are
stupendous. Thank you Julia for all your hard
work and thanks, as always go to Steve,
Peter, and Linda for such pretty photos.
And thank you, Clara and Julian.

First published in the
United States in 2009
by Ryland Peters & Small, Inc.
519 Broadway, 5th Floor
New York, NY 10012
www.rylandpeters.com

Text © Laura Washburn 2009
Design and photographs
© Ryland Peters & Small 2009

Printed in China

**Library of Congress Cataloging-in-
Publication Data**

Washburn, Laura.
  Cooking with apples and pears / Laura
Washburn ; photography by Peter Cassidy. --
1st ed.
      p. cm.
  Includes index.
  ISBN 978-1-84597-902-7
  1. Cookery (Apples) 2. Cookery (Pears) I.
Title.
  TX813.A6W383 2009
  641.6'411--dc22
                                        2009001040

10 9 8 7 6 5 4 3 2 1

Notes
• All spoon measurements are level unless
otherwise specified.
• Eggs used in the recipes in this book are
large unless specified otherwise.
• Ovens should be preheated to the
specified temperatures. All ovens work
slightly differently. We recommend using
an oven thermometer and suggest you
consult the maker's handbook for any
special instructions, particularly if you
are cooking in a fan-assisted oven, as
you will need to adjust temperatures
according to manufacturer's instructions.
• To sterilize jars, wash well in soapy water,
rinse thoroughly, then boil in plenty of water
for 10 minutes. They should be filled as soon
as they are dry, and still hot. (If the preserve
is cold, let the jar cool before filling.) For
further information on preserving visit:
http://hgic.clemson.edu/food.htm

contents

introduction

There is possibly no better subject for a cookery book than apples. They are universally liked, and have an amazing range of both sweet and savory possibilities. There are so many varieties that they offer the cook endless opportunity for experimentation. Apples are available year round and they feature prominently in many cuisines, so there is a wealth of traditional recipes to draw from.

While there are so many different types of apple, the simplest distinction is to separate into eating and cooking apple. The latter tend to be thick skinned and tart—too tart to eat almost—and often disintegrate when cooked. Eating apples are crunchy and sweet, but often lose their flavor when cooked. The most important thing is to learn about the varieties that are local to you and experiment. Quite often, the best choice is not a single type, but a combination of two or three different apples. And, depending on where you live, you might find that the supermarket isn't the only place to find apples. One thing I discovered working on the recipes for this book is that so many people I know have apple trees. Suddenly, I found myself drowning in bags full of luscious home-grown apples from everyone's gardens. It was wonderful.

And alongside apples, there are some pear recipes as these fall orchard fruits have so much in common. When it comes to choosing varieties, the same goes for types of pears; it is best to discover what is grown local to you and experiment, as varieties are abundant and all offer different flavors and textures.

But the best part about cooking with apples and pears is the smell. It is warming, comforting, and enticing. There is possibly nothing better than the aroma of orchard fruit baking in the oven. Go on, try a recipe or two and see for yourself.

savories

pear and parmesan salad with endive and walnuts

1¼ lbs. Belgian endives (about 4–5), cored, halved, and very thinly sliced

2 ripe pears, such as Williams, cored and thinly sliced

3–4 oz. Parmesan cheese, shaved

¼ cup walnuts, chopped

a handful of flatleaf parsley, finely chopped

For the vinaigrette

2 tablespoons cider vinegar

1 teaspoon fine sea salt

1 teaspoon Dijon mustard

7 tablespoons sunflower oil

1 tablespoon walnut oil (optional)

freshly ground black pepper

Serves 4

An ideal appetizer, this brings together some delicious seasonal ingredients. To obtain really thin slices of cheese, buy a chunk of Parmesan cheese and use a vegetable peeler. You can find Parmesan shavings in larger stores, but it is often more costly and the flavor is not as good.

First, prepare the vinaigrette. Put the vinegar in a bowl. Using a fork or a small whisk, stir in the salt until almost dissolved. Stir in the mustard. Stir in the oil, a tablespoon at a time, whisking well between each addition, until emulsified. (Note: If you're using the walnut oil, use 1 less tablespoon sunflower oil.) Add pepper to taste.

Just before you're ready to serve the salad, put the salad ingredients in a bowl, pour over the vinaigrette and toss gently with your hands. Divide between serving plates and serve.

1 bunch of watercress, stems trimmed, leaves rinsed and dried

2 sweet eating apples, such as Gala or Jonagold, halved, cored, and thinly sliced

1 fennel bulb, halved and thinly sliced

3 oz. Roquefort cheese, crumbled

a handful of flatleaf parsley, finely chopped

a small bunch of chives, snipped

2 cooked beets, sliced

For the vinaigrette

2 tablespoons red or white wine vinegar

1 teaspoon fine sea salt

1 teaspoon Dijon mustard

7 tablespoons sunflower oil

1 tablespoon crème fraîche or sour cream

freshly ground black pepper

Serves 4

apple, beet, and fennel salad with roquefort

This is a colorful combination of crisp ingredients that will liven up any meal. The mix of flavors and textures is very pleasing; if fennel is unavailable, you could substitute two ribs of celery, thinly sliced.

First, prepare the vinaigrette. Put the vinegar in a bowl. Using a fork or a small whisk, stir in the salt until almost dissolved. Stir in the mustard. Stir in the oil, a tablespoon at a time, whisking well between each addition, until emulsified. Finally, stir in the crème fraîche and add pepper to taste.

Just before you're ready to serve the salad, tear the watercress into pieces and put it in a bowl with the apples, fennel, cheese, parsley, and chives. Pour over all but 2 tablespoons of the vinaigrette and toss gently with your hands. Divide the salad between serving plates and top each portion with some slices of beet. Drizzle the remaining vinaigrette over the top of each and serve.

apple cole slaw

1 lb. red cabbage (about ½ a cabbage), thinly sliced

3 tablespoons red or white wine vinegar or raspberry vinegar

¼ teaspoon fine sea salt

1 lb. white cabbage (about ½ a cabbage), thinly sliced

1 cup grated carrot

1 large tart apple, such as Granny Smith, peeled, cored and coarsely grated

¼ cup pumpkin seeds, toasted

For the dressing

freshly squeezed juice of ½ an orange

1 tablespoon cider vinegar

½ teaspoon fine sea salt

1 teaspoon sugar

1 tablespoon vegetable oil

6 oz. plain yogurt (1 small pot)

¾ cup crème fraîche or sour cream

freshly ground black pepper

Serves 6–8

Plastic tubs of cole slaw are really no match for the real thing and, if you like it but have never made it yourself, you simply must. This recipe has a light creamy dressing and derives its sweetness from the apple, which makes for a delicious and healthy change.

Put the red cabbage in a heatproof bowl. Heat the wine vinegar in a small saucepan until just at a boil. Stir in the salt, then pour the mixture over the red cabbage. Toss well. This helps to set the color.

In a serving bowl, combine the red cabbage, white cabbage, carrot, and apple and toss well to combine.

To prepare the dressing, put the orange juice, vinegar, salt, and sugar in a small bowl and use a fork or small whisk to mix. Add the oil, yogurt, and crème fraîche. Mix well and season to taste with pepper.

Pour the dressing over the cabbage mixture and toss well. Taste for seasoning and adjust if necessary—it may need more salt, or more vinegar. Refrigerate for several hours before serving. When ready to serve, sprinkle with toasted pumpkin seeds. This is best eaten on the day it is prepared.

1 small onion, chopped

2 tablespoons olive oil

1 teaspoon mild curry powder

a few sprigs of fresh thyme

1 lb. parsnips (about 2–3), peeled and chopped

1 large tart cooking apple, such as Granny Smith or Bramley's, peeled, cored, and roughly chopped

5 cups chicken or vegetable stock

1 tablespoon unsalted butter

3 heaping tablespoons crème fraîche or sour cream, plus extra to serve

croûtons, to serve (optional)

sea salt and freshly ground black pepper

Serves 4

apple, parsnip, and thyme soup

Parsnips have a very distinctive taste which marries well with the sweetness of apples. In this delicious soup, the two are enhanced by a pinch of spicy curry powder and some fresh thyme. Just the thing to brighten up a dreary winter's day.

Put the onions, oil, curry powder, and a good pinch of salt in a large saucepan. Cook gently over low heat until the onions are soft. Add the thyme, parsnips, and apple and stir well. Cook for about 5 minutes, adding a little more oil if it needs it and stirring often. Add the stock and season to taste.

Simmer gently, uncovered, until the parsnips are soft, about 15–20 minutes. Purée the soup with a hand-held immersion blender, or by transferring it to a food processor and returning to the saucepan once blended. Taste and adjust the seasoning if necessary.

Stir in the butter and 3 heaping tablespoons crème fraîche and mix well. Ladle the soup into serving bowls and top with croûtons (if using) and a small dollop of crème fraîche.

bakes

pear and chocolate muffins

Pears have the fortunate ability to partner chocolate possibly better than any other fruit. In this recipe they snuggle up to lots of bittersweet chocolate and tangy cream cheese, and some cinnamon adds a pleasing spiciness.

3½ oz. bittersweet chocolate, broken into pieces

7 tablespoons unsalted butter

1 cup granulated sugar

7 oz. cream cheese (not low-fat)

2 eggs

1½ cups all-purpose flour

1½ teaspoons baking powder

1 teaspoon ground cinnamon

a pinch of fine sea salt

14 oz. ripe pears (about 2–3), such as Williams, peeled, cored, and diced

3½ oz. bittersweet chocolate chips

a 12-cup muffin pan, lined with paper liners or muffin wrappers

Makes 12 muffins

Preheat the oven to 375°F.

Put the chocolate and butter in a heatproof bowl and set it over a large saucepan of simmering water—do not let the bottom of the bowl touch the water. Stir gently as it melts. Remove the bowl from the heat just before it has melted completely and allow it to finish melting in the residual heat. Set aside until needed.

Combine the sugar and cream cheese in a mixing bowl. Beat with a hand-held electric whisk until well blended. Add the eggs and melted chocolate mixture and continue beating until well blended.

Combine all the dry ingredients in a separate bowl and mix well. Tip into the chocolate mixture and, with the whisk on low, mix until just blended. Fold in the pears and chocolate chips. Spoon the mixture into the paper liners, dividing it evenly.

Bake in the preheated oven until a skewer inserted in the center of a muffin comes out almost clean, about 20–30 minutes. Transfer to a wire rack and let cool before serving.

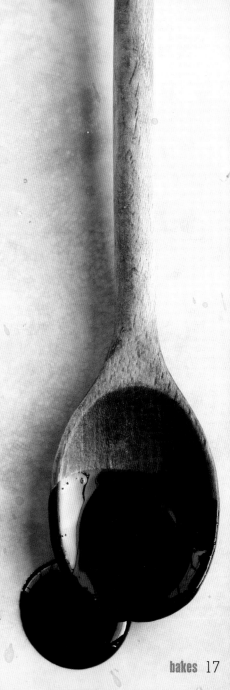

apple spice muffins

1 cup all-purpose flour

⅓ cup wholewheat flour

1 cup packed dark brown sugar

1 teaspoon baking soda

¼ teaspoon baking powder

1 teaspoon ground cinnamon

½ teaspoon each ground nutmeg, ginger, and cloves

a pinch of fine sea salt

1 cup buttermilk

½ cup vegetable oil

1 teaspoon pure vanilla extract

1 tart apple, such as Granny Smith or Jonagold, peeled, cored, and finely chopped

2 oz. raisins or golden raisins

For the frosting

2 x 8-oz. packs cream cheese (not low-fat)

1 stick unsalted butter, softened

1 cup confectioner's sugar

1 teaspoon pure vanilla extract

a 12-cup muffin pan, lined with paper liners or muffin wrappers

Makes 12 muffins

A virtuous mix of apples, raisins, wholewheat flour, buttermilk, and loads of warm spices, these muffins are perfect for breakfast, brunch, or lunch boxes. If you have fussy children who don't like bits, the apple can be coarsely grated and the raisins omitted.

To make the frosting, put the cream cheese, butter, sugar, and vanilla extract in a bowl and beat with a hand-held electric whisk until smooth. Refrigerate until needed.

Preheat the oven to 350°F. In a mixing bowl, combine the all-purpose flour, wholewheat flour, sugar, baking soda, baking powder, cinnamon, nutmeg, ginger, cloves, and salt. Mix well to combine.

In a separate bowl, combine the buttermilk, oil, and vanilla extract. Stir, then add this mixture to the dry ingredients, folding in with a spatula to blend thoroughly. Add the apple and raisins and mix just to combine.

Drop spoonfuls of the mixture into the paper liners, filling each almost to the top. Bake in the preheated oven until puffed and a skewer inserted in the center of a muffin comes out clean, about 25–35 minutes.

Transfer to a wire rack, let cool completely then spread the top of each muffin with frosting before serving.

apple dappy

This is a traditional British dessert from the West Country, little known, but highly deserving of a larger audience. It is simplicity itself to make using a food processor and uses basic pantry ingredients, a few apples, and lovely thick clotted cream if you can get some.

1 lb. tart apples, such as Cox's Orange Pippin or Granny Smith, peeled, cored, and diced

freshly squeezed juice of ½ a lemon

2 tablespoons sugar

1 tablespoon unsalted butter

For the pastry

1½ cups all-purpose flour

1 teaspoon baking powder

1 teaspoon baking soda

a pinch of fine sea salt

½ stick unsalted butter

2 tablespoons granulated sugar

2 tablespoons clotted cream or heavy cream, plus extra to serve

½ cup milk

sugar, for sprinkling

a small square or circular baking pan lined with baking parchment and lightly buttered

Serves 7

Put the apples in a saucepan with the lemon juice, sugar, and butter and cook, uncovered, over medium heat until softened. Remove from the heat and set aside.

Preheat the oven to 425°F.

In a food processor, combine the flour, baking powder, baking soda, and salt and pulse a few times to blend. Add the butter and sugar and pulse until the mixture resembles fine bread crumbs. Leave the motor on and add the cream and half of the milk. The dough should be soft and sticky. If it is too stiff, add the remaining milk.

Transfer the dough to a floured surface. You need to roll it out to a 8 x 12 inch rectangle and it should be almost exactly that, not more.

Spread the cooled apple mixture over the dough and roll up from a long end, like a jelly roll. Mark 7 equal pieces on the roll, then cut it into slices using a sharp knife. Arrange the slices, cut-side-up in the baking pan, with one in the center and the others around it. They should not actually touch as the dough will expand during baking.

Sprinkle generously with sugar and bake in the preheated oven until puffed and golden, about 20–25 minutes. Remove from the oven, let cool slightly, then serve warm with clotted cream.

applesauce cookies

When I made the Apple Butter on page 62, I only had a little left; not enough to fill a jar and too much to throw away. I devised this recipe as a way to finish it off, which proved a great success, however jarred applesauce works just as well.

5 tablespoons unsalted butter, softened

½ cup packed light brown sugar

½ cup jarred applesauce or Apple Butter (see page 62)

1 cup all-purpose flour

½ teaspoon baking soda

½ teaspoon baking powder

½ teaspoon ground cinnamon

a pinch of fine sea salt

¼ cup golden raisins or raisins

½ cup chopped nuts, such as walnuts or pecans

a baking sheet, lined with baking parchment

Makes 10–12 cookies

Preheat the oven to 400°F.

Put the butter and sugar in a mixing bowl and beat together with a hand-held electric whisk until light and fluffy. Stir in the applesauce.

In a separate bowl, combine the flour, baking soda, baking powder, cinnamon, and salt and mix well. Add the dry ingredients to the butter mixture and blend well using a wooden spoon. Add the golden raisins and nuts and fold in.

Drop walnut-size spoonfuls of the mixture at even intervals onto the prepared baking sheet. Bake in the preheated oven until the cookies are just golden around the edges but still soft, about 12–15 minutes. Transfer to a wire rack to cool. Continue baking in batches until all the mixture has been used.

The cookies can be stored in an airtight container for up to 4 days.

apple, fig, and nut bars

2 large tart apples, such as
Granny Smith, peeled, cored,
and finely chopped

2 tablespoons runny honey

2 tablespoons fresh orange juice

2 tablespoons apple juice
or water

1½ cups dried figs, finely chopped

2½ cups all-purpose flour

1 cup packed light brown sugar

1 stick plus 2 tablespoons
unsalted butter, diced

a good pinch of fine sea salt·

⅛ teaspoon ground cinnamon

1 cup pecans, hazelnuts, walnuts,
or almonds, finely chopped

*a rectangular glass or ceramic
baking dish, about 13 x 9 inches,
buttered*

Makes 16 bars

**Bars could be described as a bake that falls somewhere
between a tart and soft cookie. This filling is slightly
reminiscent of fig-centered cookies that I ate as a child
but the apples make it lighter. Good for brunch, tea time,
or cake sales, or serve warm with ice cream for dessert.**

Preheat the oven to 375°F.

In a large saucepan, combine the apples, honey, orange, and
apple juices. Set over low heat, cover and simmer gently, stirring
occasionally, until tender, about 10–15 minutes. Use a wooden spoon
to help mash the apple pieces. Add the figs and continue to simmer,
uncovered, until the figs are soft, about 5 minutes. If necessary, add
more apple juice or water if the mixture seems too thick, and use
a wooden spoon to mash to a coarse purée. Remove from the heat
and set aside to cool.

In a food processor, combine the flour, sugar, butter, salt, and
cinnamon. Pulse to obtain coarse crumbs. Alternatively, blend in
a bowl with a pastry cutter, if you have one, or use a palette knife,
then rub in using your fingers to obtain coarse crumbs.

Press half the flour mixture into the bottom of the prepared baking
dish. Spread the apple and fig mixture over the top in an even layer.
Add the nuts to the remaining flour mixture and, using your fingertips,
crumble the mixture over the apples in an even layer.

Bake in the preheated oven until browned, about 30–40 minutes. Let
cool in the baking dish, then cut into bars. The bars will keep in an
airtight container for 7–10 days.

2 sticks unsalted butter

1 cup packed light brown sugar

6 tablespoons runny honey

2 cups wholewheat flour

⅔ cup all-purpose flour

2 teaspoons baking powder

1 teaspoon cinnamon

½ teaspoon each ground cloves, ginger, and nutmeg

5 eggs, beaten

3 tablespoons ground almonds

½ cup golden raisins

1 lb. 4 oz. tart cooking apples, peeled, cored, and chopped

4 tablespoons milk

3–4 tablespoons slivered almonds, toasted

confectioner's sugar, for dusting

a cake pan, 9 inches square, buttered and lightly floured

Makes 16 squares

spiced apple cake

This cake hails from Somerset, in England, but as traditional West Country cooking can be a little spartan, I've jazzed up the basic recipe with some honey and spices.

Preheat the oven to 325°F.

Put the butter and brown sugar in a mixing bowl and cream together until light and fluffy. Beat in the honey. In a separate bowl, combine the flours, baking powder, cinnamon, cloves, ginger, and nutmeg.

Fold the dry ingredients into the butter mixture, then add the eggs and mix well using a hand-held electric whisk. Fold in the ground almonds, golden raisins, apples, and milk and mix just to combine. Transfer the mixture to the prepared pan and level the top.

Bake in the preheated oven until risen and golden and a skewer inserted in the center of the cake comes out clean, about 50 minutes. Let cool slightly in the pan then turn out onto a wire rack. When cool, sprinkle with slivered almonds and dust liberally with confectioner's sugar. Cut into squares to serve. The cake will keep in an airtight container for 4–5 days.

apple and carrot bread with walnuts

1¾ cups all-purpose flour

¾ cup light brown sugar

1 tablespoon baking powder

a pinch of fine sea salt

1 teaspoon ground cinnamon

½ teaspoon ground nutmeg

¼ teaspoon each ground ginger and allspice

⅔ cup apple juice

5 tablespoons unsalted butter, melted

2 large eggs, beaten

1 large tart cooking apple, such as Granny Smith or Bramley's, peeled, cored, and grated

1 cup grated carrots

½ cup coarsely chopped walnuts

a 9 x 5 x 4 inch loaf pan (2 lbs. capacity), buttered

Serves 6–8

This is super simple to make. One large loaf goes a long way and keeps well, so it is ideal if you just want something freshly baked around the house for a few days. It is very nice plain, or spread with butter or cream cheese if you are feeling indulgent. On my testing notes for this recipe, I had scribbled "yum yum yum". It says it all!

Preheat the oven to 350°F.

In a mixing bowl, combine the flour, sugar, baking powder, salt, cinnamon, nutmeg, ginger, and allspice. Set aside.

In a separate bowl, mix together the apple juice, melted butter, and eggs. Gently fold this mixture into the flour mixture to combine. Use your hands to squeeze every last drop of moisture from the grated apple and carrots then add to the mixture, along with the walnuts and stir just to combine.

Transfer the mixture to the prepared loaf pan and level the top. Bake in the preheated oven until a skewer inserted in the center of the cake comes out clean, about 1–1¼ hours.

Leave the cake to cool in the pan for a few minutes then turn out onto a wire rack to cool. Slice as you would bread to serve. The cake will keep in an airtight container for 4–5 days.

sweet pastry dough

1½ cups all-purpose flour
2 teaspoons granulated sugar
7 tablespoons chilled unsalted butter, cut into pieces
a pinch of fine sea salt
3–4 tablespoons cold water

a loose-bottomed tart pan, about 10½ inch diameter, buttered and lightly floured

Makes enough dough for one sweet pastry case, 10½ inch diameter

This makes enough for one large tart but the dough freezes well if carefully wrapped, so I usually make double the amount while I've got the ingredients out and am getting the food processor dirty. This way, there is always pastry dough to hand which is a great time and energy saver.

Put the flour, sugar, butter, and salt in a food processor and, using the pulse button, process until the mixture is combined (about 5–10 pulses). Add 3 tablespoons water and pulse just until the dough forms crumbs or holds together; add 1 more tablespoon if it needs it but do not do more than 10 pulses.

Transfer the dough to a piece of parchment paper, form into a ball and flatten to a circle. Wrap in the paper and let stand in a cool place for 30–60 minutes before rolling out.

Roll out the dough on a floured work surface to a circle slightly larger than the prepared tart pan. Carefully transfer the dough to the pan, patching any holes as you go and pressing gently into the sides. The sides should be slightly thicker than the bottom, but only slightly. To trim the edges, roll a rolling pin over the top, using the edge of the tin as a cutting surface and let the excess fall away. Tidy up the edges and refrigerate the pastry case until firm, at least 30 minutes.

To bake blind, preheat the oven to 400°F. Prick the pastry base all over, line with parchment paper and fill with baking weights or dried beans. Bake on a low shelf in the oven for 15 minutes, then remove the paper and weights and bake until just golden, about 10–15 minutes more. Let the pastry case cool slightly before filling.

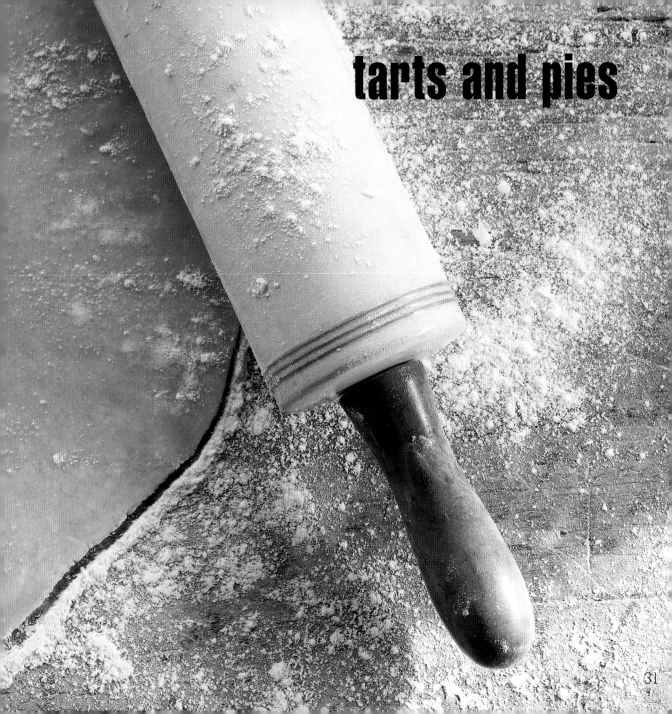

tarts and pies

apple tart

1 part-baked sweet pastry case, 10½ inches diameter (see Sweet Pastry Dough, page 30)

3 mild eating apples, such as Golden Delicious, peeled, cored, and sliced

1 tablespoon unsalted butter, melted

1 tablespoon sugar

sweetened crème fraîche, sour cream, or vanilla ice cream, to serve

For the apple and vanilla purée

3 apples (any variety), peeled, cored, and diced

1 vanilla bean, split lengthwise

2–4 tablespoons sugar, amount depends on tartness of apples

2 teaspoons unsalted butter

Serves 6–8

Apple tart is a classic but this recipe represents a slight departure. The combination of apples and vanilla is divine so I have added a layer of vanilla-scented apple purée. Serve warm or at room temperature with sweetened crème fraîche, sour cream, or vanilla ice cream.

To make the apple purée, put the diced apples, vanilla bean, sugar, and butter in a saucepan with 3–4 tablespoons water. Cook gently, stirring often until soft, adding a little more water if necessary, about 10–15 minutes. Use the tip of a small knife to scrape the seeds out of the vanilla bean, then discard the pod. Transfer the mixture to a food processor, blender, or food mill and purée until smooth.

Preheat the oven to 375°F.

Spread the purée evenly in the pastry case. Carefully arrange the apple slices in a neat circle around the edge; they should be slightly overlapping but not completely squashed together. Repeat to create an inner circle, trimming the slices slightly so that they fit, going in the opposite direction from the outer circle. Brush with melted butter and sprinkle over the sugar.

Bake in the preheated oven until just browned and tender, about 25–35 minutes. Serve warm or at room temperature with sweetened crème fraîche, sour cream, or vanilla ice cream.

tarte tatin

1 recipe Sweet Pastry Dough
(see page 30)

1 stick plus 2 tablespoons
unsalted butter

¾ cup sugar

3 lbs. Golden Delicious or tart
apples such as Granny Smith
peeled, cored, and quartered

crème fraîche or sour cream,
to serve

*a heavy flameproof tart tatin pan
(ideally enamelled cast iron or
lined copper), 7½ inches diameter*

Serves 6

Which apple variety to use for a Tarte Tatin is the source of much debate. I like to use Golden Delicious, because they hold their shape well and have a mild flavor that complements the rich caramel. Others prefer a more tart variety, but the most important thing is to use one that holds up to cooking.

Roll out the pastry on a floured work surface to a round the diameter of the pan; turn the pan upside-down on the rolled out dough and trace around it with the tip of a sharp knife. Transfer the pastry round to a baking sheet and chill until needed.

Put the butter and sugar in the tart tatin pan and set over high heat. Melt, stirring continuously to blend. Remove from the heat and arrange the apple quarters in the pan in 2 circles. The inner circle should go in the opposite direction to the outer circle.

Return to the heat and cook for about 30 minutes. From this point, watch the apples carefully and cook for a further 5–15 minutes, until the liquid thickens and turns a golden caramel color.

Preheat the oven to 400°F.

Remove the pan from the heat and top with the pastry round, gently tucking in the edges. Transfer to the preheated oven and bake until browned, about 45–60 minutes. Remove from the oven and let cool only slightly. Unmold while still warm or the caramel will harden making it too difficult. To do this, carefully invert the tart onto a serving plate so that the pastry is on the bottom. Serve hot, warm, or at room temperature with crème fraîche or sour cream.

pear and almond tart

This is a classic French pastry. Sometimes the pears are simply halved, but I think it looks more attractive if they are sliced. Vanilla ice cream or custard sauce are the best partners, but whipped cream or sour cream are good too.

1 part-baked sweet pastry case, 10½ inches diameter (see Sweet Pastry Dough page 30) or 14 x 4½ inches, as shown here

7 tablespoons unsalted butter, softened

½ cup sugar

2 large eggs

⅔ cup ground almonds

2 tablespoons all-purpose flour

seeds from ½ a vanilla bean split lengthwise, or 1 teaspoon real vanilla extract

3–4 ripe pears, such as Williams, peeled, cored, and sliced

vanilla ice cream or custard sauce, to serve

Serves 6

Preheat the oven to 375°F.

In a mixing bowl, combine the butter and sugar and beat with a hand-held electric whisk until light and fluffy. Add the eggs one at a time, beating well with each addition. Add the almonds, flour, and vanilla seeds and mix just to combine.

Spread the almond mixture in the pastry case in an even layer. Arrange the pear slices on top.

Bake in the preheated oven until puffed and golden, about 20–25 minutes. Serve warm with vanilla ice cream or custard sauce.

dutch apple pie

1 lb. 2 oz. ready-made shortcrust pastry (thawed if frozen)

3 lbs. eating apples, such as Jonagold or Golden Delicious

½ cup sugar

¾ cup golden raisins

1 teaspoon ground cinnamon

1 tablespoon freshly squeezed lemon juice

whipped cream, to serve

For the streusel topping

½ cup light brown sugar

½ cup plus 2 tablespoons all-purpose flour

1 stick unsalted butter, chilled

1 teaspoon each cinnamon, nutmeg, and allspice

a pinch of fine sea salt

½ cup chopped walnuts

a springform cake pan, 9½ inches diameter, buttered and floured

Serves 6–8

There are several different ways to top this alternative to a classic American apple pie, including a lattice crust or this streusel topping, which is not strictly speaking Dutch as it comes from the Amish communities of America.

Preheat the oven to 350°F.

Roll out the pastry on a floured work surface and line the pan with the pastry, all the way up the sides to the top edge. Let chill. Refrigerate while you prepare the apples.

Peel, core, and dice the apples and put them in a large bowl. Add the sugar, golden raisins, cinnamon, and lemon juice and mix well using your hands.

In a food processor, combine all the topping ingredients, except the walnuts, and process to form coarse crumbs. Add the walnuts and pulse a few times just to combine.

Put the apple mixture in the pastry-lined pan. Sprinkle the streusel topping over the top in an even layer, going all the way to the edges and tidy up the edges of the pastry.

Cover with foil and bake in the preheated oven for about 30 minutes. Remove the foil and continue baking until the top of the pie is golden, about 25–30 minutes.

Remove from the oven and let cool. Serve warm with whipped cream.

3 lbs. mixed apples, such as Jonagold, Honeycrisp, and Granny Smith, peeled and cored

¼ cup sugar, or more to taste

1 teaspoon ground cinnamon

1 tablespoon freshly squeezed lemon juice

light pouring cream, to serve

For the pie crust

2 cups plus 2 tablespoons all-purpose flour

1 teaspoon sugar

¼ teaspoon fine sea salt

5 tablespoons unsalted butter

5 tablespoons lard or vegetable shortening (such as Crisco)

1 egg yolk

4 tablespoons cold water

1 egg, beaten

sugar, for sprinkling

a pie dish or plate, 9 inches diameter, buttered

Serves 6–8

classic apple pie

Apple pie afficionados (me included) believe that the best pies are made with a variety of apples to combine sweet and tart flavors with firm and melting textures.

To make the pie crust, put the flour, sugar and salt in a food processor and process just to combine. Add the butter and lard and process using the pulse button until the mixture just forms coarse crumbs. Add the egg yolk and water and pulse again; the mixture should be crumbly but not holding together.

Transfer to a floured work surface and form into a ball. Cut in half, wrap well in plastic wrap and chill for at least 1 hour (if leaving longer, double wrap as the dough dries out easily). Roll out one dough half and use to line the bottom of the pie dish. Trim the edges leaving a ½ inch overhang and save the pastry trimmings for decoration if liked. Chill while you prepare the apples.

Cut the apples into slices; not too thick and not too thin. Put them in a bowl with the sugar, cinnamon, and lemon juice and use your hands to mix well. Transfer to the dough-lined pie dish.

Preheat the oven to 375°F.

Roll out the remaining dough on a floured surface to a circle large enough to cover the apples. Brush the edges of the dough in the dish with beaten egg, then lay the other pastry circle on top. Fold over the overhang from the bottom layer and crimp using your fingertips, or use the tines of a fork to seal. Decorate as desired and brush lightly with egg, then sprinkle with sugar. Cut 6–8 small slits in the top of the pie.

Put on a baking sheet and bake in the preheated oven until golden, about 50–60 minutes. Serve warm with chilled pouring cream.

praline apple strudel

Praline powder is one of my favorite secret ingredients. It's a cinch to prepare and makes a great addition to many desserts—apple or otherwise. Here it teams up with the crispy flaky phyllo pastry to lift what would be an ordinary strudel well above the average.

1 lb. tart eating apples, such as Cox's Orange Pippin, peeled, cored, and chopped

¼ cup dried fruit, such as golden raisins, cranberries, or sour cherries

½ cup packed light brown sugar

1 teaspoon ground cinnamon

1 tablespoon unsalted butter

6 sheets phyllo pastry (thawed if frozen)

4 tablespoons unsalted butter, melted

confectioner's sugar, to dust

whipped cream, crème fraîche, or sour cream, to serve

For the praline

½ cup shelled pecans

¼ cup sugar

a baking sheet lined with baking parchment

Serves 6–8

To make the praline, combine the pecans and sugar in a non-stick heavy-based skillet and cook over medium/high heat, stirring constantly, until the sugar hardens and coats the nuts. Transfer to a plate to cool, then process in a coffee grinder or small food processor until ground to a coarse powder. Set aside.

In a large saucepan, combine the apples, dried fruit, brown sugar, cinnamon, and 1 tablespoon butter. Cook over medium heat until the apples are soft and the juices have evaporated, about 15 minutes. Remove from the heat and let cool.

Preheat the oven to 375°F.

Put 2 sheets of phyllo on the prepared baking sheet and brush with some melted butter. Sprinkle with a little praline. Top with 2 more sheets of phyllo and repeat. Top with 2 more sheets of phyllo. Spread the apple mixture in an even layer over the top sheet of phyllo. Sprinkle with more praline mixture, then carefully roll up from a long end, like a jelly roll. Use the paper to help you roll, if necessary. The seam side needs to be on the bottom. Brush with a little more melted butter, sprinkle with any remaining praline and bake in the preheated oven until crisp and golden, about 25–35 minutes.

Remove from the oven and let cool slightly. Dust with a little confectioner's sugar, slice, and serve warm with whipped cream, crème fraîche, or sour cream.

desserts

apple and blackberry crumble

There is no better partner for apples than ripe, juicy blackberries. This easy dessert is simply divine served warm from the oven with a scoop of vanilla ice cream.

2 lbs. mixed apple varieties, peeled, cored, and chopped
1 lb. blackberries
¼ cup sugar
vanilla ice cream, to serve

For the crumble topping

1 cup porridge oats
1 cup all-purpose flour
½ cup packed light brown sugar
½ cup ground almonds
½ teaspoon ground cinnamon
1 stick plus 2 tablespoons unsalted butter, cut into cubes

an ovenproof dish, 9–10 inches diameter or 4–6 individual dishes, 3½– 4½ inches diameter, well-buttered

Serves 4–6

Preheat the oven to 400°F.

Put the apples, berries, and sugar in a mixing bowl and use your hands to mix well. Transfer to the prepared baking dish.

To prepare the crumble topping, combine the oats, flour, sugar, almonds, and cinnamon in a bowl and mix well. Add the butter. Using a pastry blender, or your fingertips, rub in the butter until the mixture resembles coarse breadcrumbs. Alternatively, use a food processor and blend carefully with the pulse button; do not over-process or you will grind the oats too finely.

Sprinkle the topping evenly over the apple mixture. Bake in the preheated oven until the crumble is golden and the fruit is bubbling up underneath, about 35–45 minutes. Serve warm with vanilla ice cream.

apple brown betty with dried cranberries

2 lbs. tart apples, such as Cox's Orange Pippin or Granny Smith, peeled, cored, and diced

1 teaspoon ground cinnamon

1 tablespoon finely grated orange peel

⅓ cup apple or orange juice

⅔ cup dried cranberries

3 cups fresh white bread crumbs

6 tablespoons unsalted butter, melted

⅔ cup chopped pecans

½ cup light brown sugar

2 tablespoons unsalted butter, chilled

whipped cream, to serve

a non-stick baking dish, about 8 inches diameter, well-buttered

Serves 4–6

This is another traditional American recipe with very humble origins. It is always made with apples but not necessarily dried cranberries. Just like English bread pudding, it is an economic way to use up stale bread but I have found that it tastes even better if you use fresh white bread or even brioche.

Preheat the oven to 375°F.

In a bowl, combine the apples, cinnamon, grated orange peel, apple juice, and cranberries. Toss gently with your hands to mix and set aside.

In a separate bowl, combine the bread crumbs and melted butter and mix well.

Spread about one-third of the buttered bread crumbs in the bottom of the prepared baking dish. Add the pecans and sugar to the remaining bread crumbs and mix to combine.

Put half of the apple mixture on top of the bread crumbs in the baking dish. Top with half the bread crumb and pecan mixture. Top this with the remaining apple mixture and finish with the remainder of the bread crumb and pecan mixture. Dot with the chilled butter and bake in the preheated oven until golden, about 30–40 minutes. Serve warm with whipped cream.

pear cobbler

1½ lbs. pears, peeled, cored, and sliced

¼ cup light brown sugar

2 tablespoons all-purpose flour

1 teaspoon real vanilla extract

finely grated peel of 1 orange

vanilla ice cream or whipped cream, to serve

For the cobbler batter

2 cups all-purpose flour

1 cup sugar

1 tablespoon baking powder

a pinch of fine sea salt

1 cup milk

1 stick plus 1 tablespoon unsalted butter, melted

extra sugar or cinnamon sugar, to sprinkle

an ovenproof baking dish, about 9–10 inches diameter, well-buttered

Serves 4–6

A cobbler is a dessert consisting of a sweetened thick batter poured over fruit and baked. Other names for similar recipes are grunt, slump, and buckle, but they are all pretty much the same thing. It is a homey dish, easy to make and even easier to eat!

Preheat the oven to 375°F.

In a bowl, combine the pears, sugar, flour, vanilla extract, and grated orange peel. Toss gently with your hands to combine and arrange in an even layer in the bottom of the prepared baking dish. Set aside.

To prepare the cobbler batter, combine the flour, sugar, baking powder, and salt in a separate bowl. In a third bowl, stir together the milk and melted butter. Gradually pour the milk mixture into the dry ingredients, beating with a wooden spoon until just smooth.

Drop spoonfuls of the batter on top of the pears, leaving gaps but spreading to the edges. Sprinkle the top with sugar and bake in the preheated oven until golden brown, about 40–50 minutes. Serve warm with vanilla ice cream or whipped cream.

pear and fig clafoutis with almonds

3 ripe pears

3 ripe figs

¾ cup crème fraîche or sour cream

¾ cup milk

3 eggs

¾ cup sugar

2 tablespoons ground almonds

½ teaspoon ground cinnamon

confectioner's sugar, to dust

light pouring cream, to serve

an ovenproof dish, 9–10 inches diameter, well-buttered

Serves 4–6

This delicious dessert is ideal for entertaining because it looks fantastic but is very easy to prepare. Simply make the batter and prepare the fruit in advance, then combine the two and put in the oven at the start of the meal. It will be done just when you are ready to serve.

Preheat the oven to 400°F.

Peel and core the pears and cut into largeish pieces. Trim the stem ends from the figs and cut into slightly smaller pieces. If there is too much white on the skins, trim this off. Put the fruit in the prepared baking dish and distribute evenly. Set aside.

In a mixing bowl, combine the crème fraîche, milk, eggs, sugar, almonds, and cinnamon. Mix well with a hand-held electric whisk.

Pour the batter evenly over the fruit and bake in the preheated oven until puffed and golden, about 35–45 minutes. Let cool slightly and dust with confectioner's sugar just before serving. Serve warm with chilled pouring cream.

2 apples, preferably Cox's Orange Pippin or Braeburn

1 just-ripe pear, preferably Conference

2 tablespoons chopped hazelnuts

1 tablespoon golden raisins

4–5 dried apricots, chopped

ground cinnamon, to dust

2 tablespoons unsalted butter

runny honey, to drizzle

plain Greek yogurt, to serve

a non-stick baking dish, large enough to comfortably hold the fruit

Serves 2

baked apples and pears with dried fruit, honey, and hazelnuts

Baked fruit is both easy on the cook and easy on the waistline. This recipe gives quantities for two servings to make it simple to increase as needed. I like to serve these with a dollop of plain, unsweetened Greek yogurt.

Preheat the oven to 400°F.

Peel the apples. If necessary, trim the bottoms slightly so that they sit flat. Using a small knife or a corer, remove the cores. With a small spoon, scrape out some apple around the core cavity to allow for more stuffing. Peel the pear, halve, and scoop out the core, as for the apple.

In a bowl, mix together the hazelnuts, golden raisins and apricots.

Arrange the apples and pears in the baking dish. Stuff the nut mixture into the apple and pear cavities, mounding it at the top. Top each with a light sprinkling of cinnamon and a good knob of butter, then drizzle each with 1–2 teaspoons of honey, to taste. Cover with foil.

Bake in the preheated oven for 20 minutes, then remove the foil and continue baking until just golden, about 10–15 minutes. Divide the apples and pears carefully between serving plates and pour over any pan juices. Serve warm with plain Greek yogurt.

poached pears

These glistening crimson pears make a lovely simple ending to a rich meal. They are a very good choice for entertaining as they should be made in advance so that they have time to marinate in the poaching liquid and take on their gorgeous jewel-like color.

In a saucepan large enough to hold the pears standing upright, combine the wine, sugar, honey, lemon juice, cinnamon stick, vanilla bean, orange peel, clove, and peppercorn. Warm over low heat, stirring occasionally until the sugar has dissolved. Remove from the heat.

Peel the pears but leave them whole.

Place the pears in the wine mixture and simmer, uncovered, until tender (test with the tip of a sharp knife). Timing depends on the quantity, size, and ripeness of the pears, about 20–35 minutes.

Transfer the pears to a shallow, non-reactive bowl using a large slotted spoon. Continue cooking the poaching liquid over medium heat until it has reduced by half. Let cool, then strain it through a strainer and pour over the pears. Leave the pears in the liquid, turning them occasionally, for at least 3 hours before serving.

Note: This dessert can be made up to several days in advance and kept refrigerated. Return the pears to room temperature before serving.

750 ml (1 bottle) good red wine
¾ cup sugar
3 tablespoons runny honey
freshly squeezed juice of 1 lemon
1 cinnamon stick
1 vanilla bean, split lengthwise
1 large piece of orange peel
1 whole clove
1 black peppercorn
4–6 firm pears
sweetened crème fraîche, sour cream, whipped cream, or vanilla ice cream, to serve

Serves 4–6

10 oz. genoese sponge (about one 9–10-inch cake)

4 tablespoons cognac (optional)

4–6 poached pears (see page 55) poaching liquid reserved

1 cup whipping cream, whipped

toasted slivered almonds, to top

For the custard

1 cup milk

¼ cup heavy cream

8 egg yolks

½ cup sugar

1 vanilla bean,
split lengthwise
or 1 teaspoon real
vanilla extract

*a glass serving dish
or 4–6 individual
serving dishes*

Serves 4–6

spiced pear trifle

Trifle is a traditional English dessert but this recipe departs from the classic recipe as it uses spiced poached pears instead of canned peaches. It is easy to make and looks spectacular when assembled in a large glass bowl.

To make the custard, combine the milk and cream in a saucepan and warm over low heat. Meanwhile, whisk together the egg yolks and sugar in a heatproof bowl. Whisk the warm milk mixture into the egg yolk mixture, then return the mixture to the saucepan, stirring constantly with a wooden spoon, until it thickens. As soon as it thickens, remove from the heat, transfer to a bowl and scrap in the vanilla seeds from the pod. Stir them into the custard. Cover the surface of the custard closely with greaseproof paper to prevent a skin from forming and set aside to cool.

When you're ready to serve, cut the sponge cake into pieces and arrange these in the bottom of the serving dish. Drizzle with the cognac (if using) and some reserved pear poaching liquid. Top with the quartered pears, then spoon over some of the custard. Spoon the whipped cream on top, sprinkle with the almonds and serve.

chutneys and jellies

chutneys

Homemade chutneys are a great thing to keep on hand. They are ideal served with a selection of cheeses and crackers, as part of a ploughman's lunch, and they are perfect with roast meats—both hot and cold. They also make a nice sandwich ingredient. The Apple, Pear, and Ginger Chutney is especially suited to pork, and the Apple, Red Onion, and Cherry Chutney goes very well with chicken, turkey, and even duck.

apple, pear, and ginger chutney

3 eating apples, such as Golden Delicious, peeled, cored, and diced

2 large ripe pears, peeled, cored, and diced

1 large white onion, finely chopped

1½ cups cider vinegar

1½ cups light brown sugar

¾ cup golden raisins or raisins

5-oz. piece of fresh ginger, peeled and finely chopped

½ teaspoon sea salt

½ teaspoon dried hot pepper flakes

Makes 4–5 cups

In a large non-reactive saucepan, combine the apples, pears, onion, vinegar, sugar, golden raisins, ginger, salt, and hot pepper flakes. Cook over medium heat, stirring occasionally, until thick, about 30–40 minutes.

Transfer the chutney to a spotlessly clean and dry, sealable airtight container. It will keep in the fridge for up to 2 weeks.

apple, red onion, and cherry chutney

3 eating apples, such as Golden Delicious, peeled, cored, and diced

1 large or 2 medium red onions, halved and sliced

1 heaping cup dried sour cherries

2 cups cider vinegar

3 tablespoons light brown sugar

¼ teaspoon ground cloves

¼ teaspoon sea salt

freshly ground black pepper

Makes 2–3 cups

In a large non-reactive saucepan, combine the apples, onion, dried cherries, vinegar, sugar, cloves, salt, and a few grinds of black pepper. Cook over medium heat, stirring occasionally, until thick, about 30–40 minutes.

Transfer the chutney to a spotlessly clean and dry, sealable airtight container. It will keep in the fridge for up to 2 weeks.

roasted pear relish

A fantastic accompaniment to roast pork and poultry or bread with sharp cheddar.

4 ripe pears, peeled, halved, and cored
2 tablespoons freshly squeezed lemon juice
1 tablespoon light brown sugar
¼ cup sugar
¾ teaspoon ground cinnamon
¼ teaspoon ground cloves
¼ cup pure maple syrup
1 small red onion, cut into ½-inch slices
1 tablespoon peeled and grated fresh ginger
5 tablespoons raisins
½ cup cider vinegar
1 teaspoon dried hot pepper flakes (optional)
vegetable oil, for brushing

Serves 4–6

Preheat the oven to 350°F.

Brush a baking sheet with vegetable oil. In a bowl, combine the pears, lemon juice, both the sugars, cinnamon, and cloves and mix well to coat the pears. Arrange the pears cut-side down on the sheet and brush with a little more oil. Roast in the preheated oven until caramelized, about 45 minutes. When the pears are cool enough to handle, cut into small cubes.

Meanwhile, put all the remaining ingredients in a non-reactive saucepan and bring to a boil. Reduce the heat and simmer, uncovered, for 5 minutes. Remove from the heat and let cool. Add the cubed pears to the onion mixture and mix well. Cover and refrigerate for at least 1 day before serving. Transfer the relish to a spotlessly clean and dry, sealable airtight container. It will keep in the fridge for up to 10 days.

apple jelly

This is delicious without any flavorings, but adding fresh sage makes it perfect for brushing over pork as it roasts. Elderflower with apple is a quintessentially English combination and worth trying if you are able to find elderflowers when they are in season.

6 lbs. tart cooking apples, such as
Granny Smith or Suncrisp
sugar, as required (see method below)
freshly squeezed juice of 1 lemon, strained
fresh sage leaves or elderflowers (optional)

Makes about 6 lbs.

Slice the apples but do not peel or core. Put the apple slices in a large non-reactive saucepan and add water to cover. Add the elderflowers at this point, if using. Cook over medium heat until soft, about 30–40 minutes, and then let stand overnight.

The next day, prepare a nylon jelly bag or, if you don't have one, boil a kitchen towel in a large saucepan of water for 2–3 minutes, wring well, and leave to cool before using. Set the bag or kitchen towel over a bowl, pour in the apple mixture and let it slowly drip through; do not stir or squeeze the bag.

Measure the juice, then transfer it to a separate clean non-reactive saucepan. Simmer, uncovered, for about 5 minutes, skimming off any foam that rises to the surface. For each 1 cup apple liquid you'll need to add ¾–1 cup sugar. Stir until dissolved.

Boil until setting point; the jelly will turn a darker amber color. Stir in the lemon juice and pour into hot, dry sterilized jars (see note on page 4). Add a few sage leaves, if using. Let cool, then seal. The jelly will keep for 3–4 weeks if correctly sealed.

apple and cranberry sauce

This is a classic fruit sauce to accompany turkey, goose, or roast pork. A good pinch of ground cloves and a dash of balsamic vinegar during cooking will dress it up for Christmas.

one 12-oz package fresh cranberries
1 large tart cooking apple, such as Granny Smith, peeled, cored, and chopped
⅓ cup dried apricots, chopped
¾ cup sugar
4 tablespoons freshly squeezed orange juice

Serves 4–6

Combine all the ingredients in a large non-reactive saucepan and cook over medium heat, stirring often. Add a little water if the mixture seems dry. The cranberries will pop as they cook, which is fine.

Cook until the fruit has softened and the mixture is thick, about 15–20 minutes. Remove from the heat. Taste for sweetness; add more sugar if desired. Transfer the sauce to a spotlessly clean and dry, sealable airtight container. It will keep in the fridge for 3–4 days. Bring to room temperature to serve.

apple pumpkin jelly

This is an unusual and delicious conserve, and a handy Autumn recipe as it offers a use for retired Halloween jack o'lanterns.

2 lbs. pumpkin, peeled, seeded, and diced
2 lbs. tart cooking apples, such as Granny Smith, peeled, cored, and chopped
freshly squeezed juice of ½ a lemon
500 g sugar
1 teaspoon ground ginger

Makes about 3½ lbs.

Put all the ingredients in a large non-reactive saucepan. Cook over medium heat, covered, for about 5–10 minutes to release the juices, then remove the lid and lower the heat.

Simmer for 40–50 minutes, stirring occasionally, and mashing the apples and pumpkin with a wooden spoon to break up the bigger pieces.

Let cool, then transfer the jelly to a spotlessly clean and dry, sealable airtight container. It will keep in the fridge for up to 10 days.

apple blackberry jelly

This fruity jelly is unbelievably simple to make but extraordinarily delicious.

4½ cups blackberries
3 medium cooking apples, such as Granny Smith, peeled, cored, and chopped
2 cups sugar
1 tablespoon freshly squeezed lemon juice

Makes about 1 quart

Combine the blackberries, apples, sugar, and lemon juice in a large non-reactive saucepan. Cook over medium heat, stirring, until the sugar dissolves.

Continue cooking, stirring occasionally, until the fruit softens, about 20–30 minutes. Use a wooden spoon to crush the fruit slightly as you stir. Remove from the heat. Transfer the jelly to a spotlessly clean and dry, sealable airtight container. It will keep in the fridge for 7–10 days.

apple butter

Use this deliciously appley treat as you would any fruit jelly; spread on toast, with brioche, in sandwiches, drizzled over pancakes, or as a filling for pound cakes.

3 lbs. mixed apples, such as Braeburn, Cox's Orange Pippin, and Granny Smith, peeled, cored, and chopped
¾ cup runny honey
1 cup sugar
2 tablespoons freshly squeezed lemon juice
1 teaspoon ground cinnamon
½ teaspoon ground cloves
1 cup apple juice

Makes about 3½ lbs.

Combine all the ingredients in a large non-reactive saucepan. Bring to a boil, stirring occasionally. Lower the heat and simmer, stirring occasionally, and using a wooden spoon, crush the apples, until thick, about 20–25 minutes. Remove from the heat.

Transfer the apple butter to a spotlessly clean and dry, sealable airtight container. It will keep in the fridge for 7–10 days. Alternatively, spoon into hot, dry sterilized jars while hot (see note on page 4). Let cool, then seal. The butter will keep for 3–4 weeks if correctly sealed.

conversion chart

The recipes in this book require the following conversions. Please note that weights and measures have been rounded up or down to make measuring easier.

Measuring butter:

A US stick of butter weighs 4 oz. which is approximately 115 g or 8 tablespoons.

American	Metric	Imperial
1 tbsp	85 g	3 oz.
7 tbsp	100 g	3½ oz.
1 stick	115 g	4 oz.

Volume equivalents:

American	Metric	Imperial
1 teaspoon	5 ml	
1 tablespoon	15 ml	
¼ cup	60 ml	2 fl.oz.
⅓ cup	75 ml	2½ fl.oz.
½ cup	125 ml	4 fl.oz.
⅔ cup	150 ml	5 fl.oz. (¼ pint)
¾ cup	175 ml	6 fl.oz.
1 cup	250 ml	8 fl.oz.

Weight equivalents:		**Measurements:**	
Imperial	Metric	Inches	Cm
1 oz.	30 g	¼ inch	0.5 cm
2 oz.	55 g	½ inch	1 cm
3 oz.	85 g	¾ inch	1.5 cm
3½ oz.	100 g	1 inch	2.5 cm
4 oz.	115 g	2 inches	5 cm
5 oz.	140 g	3 inches	7 cm
6 oz.	175 g	4 inches	10 cm
8 oz. (½ lb.)	225 g	5 inches	12 cm
9 oz.	250 g	6 inches	15 cm
10 oz.	280 g	7 inches	18 cm
11½ oz.	325 g	8 inches	20 cm
12 oz.	350 g	9 inches	23 cm
13 oz.	375 g	10 inches	25 cm
14 oz.	400 g	11 inches	28 cm
15 oz.	425 g	12 inches	30 cm
16 oz. (1 lb.)	450 g